U.S. SPECIAL OPS FORCES

JEN BESEL

BLACK RABBIT BOOKS

Bolt Jr. is published by Black Rabbit Books
P.O. Box 227, Mankato, Minnesota, 56002
www.blackrabbitbooks.com

Michael Sellner, designer and photo researcher

Library of Congress Cataloging-in-Publication Data
Names: Besel, Jennifer M., author.
Title: U.S. Special Ops forces / by Jen Besel.
Description: Mankato, Minnesota : Black Rabbit Books, [2023] | Series: Bolt Jr. mighty military | Includes bibliographical references and index. | Audience: Ages 6-8 | Audience: Grades K-1 | Summary: "Engage young readers with information about United States' special operations forces. From Navy SEALs to Army Rangers, readers will learn all about the different groups that secretly protect the United States." -- Provided by publisher.
Identifiers: LCCN 2021056825 (print) | LCCN 2021056826 (ebook) | ISBN 9781623107659 (hardcover) | ISBN 9781644665923 (paperback) | ISBN 9781623107710 (ebook)
Subjects: LCSH: Special forces (Military science)--United States--Juvenile literature. | Special operations (Military science)--United States--Juvenile literature.
Classification: LCC UA34.S64 B475 2023 (print) | LCC UA34.S64 (ebook) | DDC 356/.160973--dc23/eng/20211123
LC record available at https://lccn.loc.gov/2021056825
LC ebook record available at https://lccn.loc.gov/2021056826

Image Credits

Alamy: AB Forces News Collection, 17; US Navy Photo, 20; Dreamstime: Roman Kanin, 11; Ultraone, 13; gary's mod: Stefano96, 8–9; iStock: zabelin, Cover; Shutterstock: CreativeHQ, 10; Dzmitry Kim, 3; Getmilitaryphotos, 1, 18–19; Hafiz Hamza Nisar, 6–7; iamseki, 14–15; santoelia, 4; U.S. Air Force: Staff Sgt. Jeremy T. Lock, 5; U.S. Army: AFP, 12–13; U.S. Navy: Chief Photographer's Mate Andrew McKaskle, 22–23; Wikimedia Commons: Airwolfhound, 21; USSOCOM, 7

Contents

CHAPTER 1

What Are Special Ops Forces?

They jump from planes in the night. They sneak into enemy lands. They place underwater **bombs**. Sometimes the United States needs fast, secret jobs done. Special ops teams are ready.

bomb: a weapon that explodes

COMPARING ARMY RANGERS' WEAPONS

Important Teams

The U.S. military has many special ops teams. Some teams, like Army Rangers, attack on land. Other teams do air missions. Some, like Navy SEALs, work in the water.

Mk 48 machine gun
fires about 730 rounds per minute

EXPLORING A

SEAL Delivery Vehicle

doors
propeller
passenger
space

CHAPTER 2

Land Teams

Green Berets fight in small teams. They surprise enemies. This group often saves **hostages**.

hostage: a person captured by an enemy

FACT

Green Berets are part of the Army.

Army Rangers

Army Rangers is another special ops group. This group is always ready to travel fast. Rangers take over enemy **runways**.

runway: a strip of ground used for the landing and takeoff of airplanes

Where Special Ops Forces Have Worked

Europe
Asia
Africa
Australia

CHAPTER 3

Air and Sea Teams

Air Commandos jump from planes. They land in enemy areas. They rescue hurt soldiers.

FACT
Commandos are part of the Air Force.

Navy SEALs

SEALs often attack from the water. Members must be very strong swimmers.

Special ops teams do many jobs. They are always ready to keep the United States safe.

How Many People Finish SEAL Training

20 percent

Bonus Facts

In training, SEALs swim with their arms and legs tied.

Less than half of the people who try pass Ranger school.

Sometimes, teams train soldiers from other countries.

Green Beret is a nickname. The team is the U.S. Army Special Forces.

nickname: a usually descriptive name given in addition to a person or group's formal name

READ MORE/WEBSITES

Colins, Luke. *U.S. Special Ops Forces.* U.S. Military Forces. Mankato, MN: Black Rabbit Books, 2021.

Leed, Percy. *The U.S. Army in Action.* U.S. Military Branches. Minneapolis: Lerner Publications, 2023.

Phillips, Howard. *Inside the Navy SEALs.* U.S. Special Ops Forces. New York: PowerKids Press, 2022.

United States Army Rangers
www.army.mil/ranger/

U.S. Navy SEAL Careers
www.navy.com/careers/navy-seal

GLOSSARY

bomb (BAHM)—a weapon that explodes

hostage (HAHS-tij)—a person captured by an enemy

nickname (NIK-nayhm)—a usually descriptive name given in addition to a person or group's formal name

runway (RUN-way)—a strip of ground used for the landing and takeoff of airplanes

INDEX